A POT FULL OF TALES

Using Folk Tales to Teach Creative Thinking and Writing

Written by Vowery Dodd Carlile
Illustrated by Karen Neulinger
and James Uttel

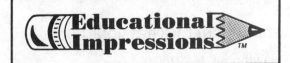

ISBN 1-56644-972-3
© 1994 Educational Impressions, Inc., Hawthorne, NJ

Printed in the U.S.A.

EDUCATIONAL IMPRESSIONS, INC.

Hawthorne, NJ 07507

Contents

FOREWORD

Folk tales have always been an exciting part of my life. I enjoyed listening to them when I was young and I enjoy teaching them to my students now.

I believe that students can learn valuable lessons from folk tales. Each has a moral-of-the-story type attitude that gently runs throughout the story. When students see the consequences of the characters' decisions, they often relate the characters' problems to their own and learn from the characters' mistakes. Rather than lecture students about right and wrong, it's fun to see them reach their own conclusions through the reading of the tales.

A Pot Full of Tales: Using Folk Tales to Teach Creative Thinking and Writing presents ten popular folk tales, which are used to teach creative thinking and writing. Each unit begins with a summary of the story and questions from Bloom's *Taxonomy.** Following these questions are independent project ideas developed to encourage creative thinking and writing.

The units may be used in any order. Begin each by reading the story to the class. Ask any or all Bloom questions based upon the story. Then choose some or all of the projects for the students to complete.

After all the books have been read, allow the children to do the puzzles and other activities and to play the "Folk Tale Magic" game. This game asks questions about all the folk tales included in the book and provides a fun way to review and end the unit.

I really enjoyed writing this book. It gave me the opportunity to re-read many of my younger-day favorite folk tales. I would like to thank my wonderful husband, Gene, for his creativity and help in choosing a title for this book.

Vowery Dodd Carlile

* Benjamin Bloom, *Taxonomy of Educational Objectives*, (New York: David McKay Company, Inc., 1956).

INTRODUCTION

A Pot Full of Tales: Using Folk Tales to Teach Creative Thinking and Writing uses favorite folk tales to teach children to read, think, and write critically and creatively. Storytellers made their living traveling from one town to another, spreading their tales as they entertained audiences. Because the stories weren't written down, they often changed each time they were told. The tellers used their creativity and imagination to make the stories even more exciting each time they were repeated!

These tales were passed down from one generation to the next. Today, too, stories are often told before they are written down. Tales told by family members today may become the folk tales of the future.

Stories require several elements to be categorized as folk tales. A true folk tale needs imagination, repetition, and both real and make-believe characters and events. Throughout the reading of these tales, these elements should be elicited from the students and eventually recognized by them on their own. Doing a story map of the folk tales may be helpful. (See the sample below.) By the time the students have worked through several of the tales, they should be able to write their own folk tales. The organizational sheet in the latter part of the book should help youngsters organize their stories.

SAMPLE STORY MAP OF *THE THREE LITTLE PIGS*

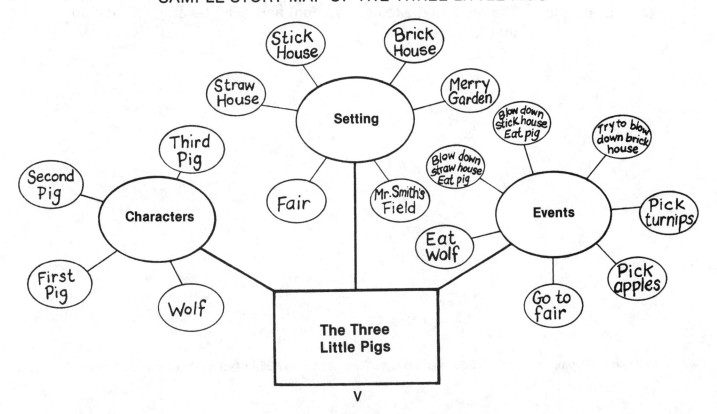

An important part of each unit is the series of questions and activities based upon Bloom's *Taxonomy of Educational Objectives.** Bloom divided cognitive development into six main levels: knowledge, comprehension, application, analysis, synthesis, and evaluation. Most of the questions presented to students fall into the first two categories, knowledge and comprehension. The highest levels are seldom used; they are more difficult to write and, because they have no definite answer, are more difficult to evaluate. The following is a brief description of the cognitive levels according to Bloom's taxonomy.

Knowledge: This level involves the **simple recall** of facts stated directly.

Comprehension: The student must **understand** what has been read at this level. It will not be stated directly.

Application: The student uses knowledge that has been learned and **applies** it to a new situation. He/She must understand that knowledge in order to use it.

Analysis: The student **breaks down** learned knowledge into small parts and analyzes it. He/She will pick out unique characteristics and compare them with other ideas.

Synthesis: The student can now **create** something new and original from the acquired knowledge. This level involves a great deal of creativity.

Evaluation: The student makes a **judgment** and must be able to back up that judgment.

* Benjamin Bloom, *Taxonomy of Educational Objectives,* (New York: David McKay Company, Inc., 1956).

The shape activities are another integral part of each unit. They are designed to promote higher-level creative-thinking skills. These activities can be used as class or independent projects.

Independent projects can be written to cover any subject using verbs that encourage responses from each of the six categories. Verbs for each of the categories include the following:

Knowledge: list, know, define, relate, repeat, recall, specify, tell, name

Comprehension: recognize, restate, explain, describe, summarize, express, review, discuss, identify, locate, report, retell

Application: demonstrate, interview, simulate, dramatize, experiment, show, use, employ, operate, exhibit, apply, calculate, solve, illustrate

Analysis: compare, examine, categorize, group, test, inventory, probe, analyze, discover, arrange, scrutinize, organize, contrast, classify, survey

Synthesis: plan, develop, invent, predict, propose, produce, arrange, formulate, construct, incorporate, originate, create, prepare, design, set up

Evaluation: value, recommend, evaluate, criticize, estimate, decide, conclude, predict, judge, compare, rate, measure, select, infer

These verbs can be used to design independent projects as well as to write your own higher-level questions in any subject area. Below is an example of the chart that I use when creating the independent projects in my books. I have also included a copy for you to reproduce and use when designing your own projects.

CATEGORY	VERB	TOPIC	PROJECT
Synthesis	Create	Jack and the Beanstalk	Another treasure that Jack might bring back from the giant.

By incorporating these question-and-project strategies into the curriculum, every child will be given the opportunity to be a creative thinker.

Independent Projects Chart

CATEGORY	VERB	TOPIC	PROJECT

The Golden Goose

The Golden Goose

by the Brothers Grimm

STORY SUMMARY

Long ago there lived a woodcutter and his wife; they had three sons. The elder sons despised the youngest one and thought him stupid; they called him Simpleton.

One day the eldest son went out into the woods to chop wood. His mother gave him some sweet cake and wine for the journey. In the woods he met a little old man, who asked him to share his provisions. But the eldest son refused, saying that there wouldn't be enough for him. As soon as he began to chop the wood, he accidentally (or so he thought!) cut his arm with his ax and had to return home.

The second son went into the woods to complete the task his brother had begun. He, too, had been given sweet cake and wine by his mother. When he got into the woods, the same little old man approached him and asked him to share his food and wine. This brother also refused, giving the same excuse as the first. When he began to chop the wood, he cut his leg; like his brother, he went home without completing his task.

Simpleton begged his father to let him go into the forest to cut the wood. At first his father refused; however, he finally agreed, thinking it would teach him a lesson. Simpleton's mother gave him some cake that had been baked in the ashes and some sour beer.

When Simpleton arrived in the forest, he met the little old man. The little man asked him to share what he had, and Simpleton did so gladly. The cake baked in ashes turned into a beautiful sweet cake and the sour beer became fine wine. What's more, the man told Simpleton that if he cut down an old tree, it would bring him good luck.

Simpleton did as he was told and found a goose with feathers of gold. He put the goose under his arm and set out to make his fortune. On the way he stopped at an inn to eat and sleep. The innkeeper had three daughters, each of whom wanted one of the golden feathers. During the night they sneaked into Simpleton's room. The first sister reached for the goose and could not pull away. The second reached for the first and she, too, was held fast. The third reached for the second and she also became stuck!

The next morning Simpleton left the inn, not realizing that he was dragging the three girls behind him. An old parson saw them and tried to stop the girls. The parson also got stuck. Soon the sexton passed by and tried to pull the parson off, but the sexton, too, became stuck in the procession. Finally, two farmers tried to pull everyone off and they, too, became stuck. Of course, Simpleton still had no idea of the commotion he was causing.

It so happened that nearby lived a lovely princess who hadn't laughed in three years. Her father, the king, said that whoever could make her laugh would win her hand in marriage. When the princess saw Simpleton and his strange procession, she burst out laughing. Not wanting anyone called Simpleton to marry his daughter, the king insisted upon all sorts of conditions. Each time the little old man helped Simpleton fulfill them. Finally, the king consented. Simpleton and the princess were married and lived happily ever after.

Note: There are different versions of this story. You might want to have the children read more than one version and compare them.

Questions & Activities Based Upon Bloom's Taxonomy

The Golden Goose

Knowledge:
1. How many sons did the woodcutter have?
2. Why was the youngest son called Simpleton?
3. What did the little old man want from the brothers?

Comprehension:
1. Why did Simpleton's brothers have bad luck?
2. How did Simpleton's food and drink change? Who made this happen?
3. Why did the three sisters stick to the goose?

Application:
1. Explain what a parson is.
2. Typically, folk tales have repeated lines or action. Describe the repeated lines or action in this folk tale.
3. Suppose you saw Simpleton and his followers. How might you have reacted?

Analysis:
1. What other story has a golden goose? How do these two stories compare?
2. Compare the three brothers. How are they alike and how are they different?
3. What is the moral of this story?

Synthesis:
1. Suppose you had to make the princess laugh or lose your life. How might you accomplish this task?
2. Create a way to get the people unstuck from the goose without hurting them or the goose. Tell about it.
3. Predict what kind of life Simpleton will have now that he is married to the princess.

Evaluation:
1. As Simpleton, write a letter to your mother explaining how you feel about the way your family treated you.
2. Did Simpleton's brothers deserve what happened to them? Explain.
3. Do you think this folk tale ended well? If so, tell why; if not, explain how you would have ended it.

3

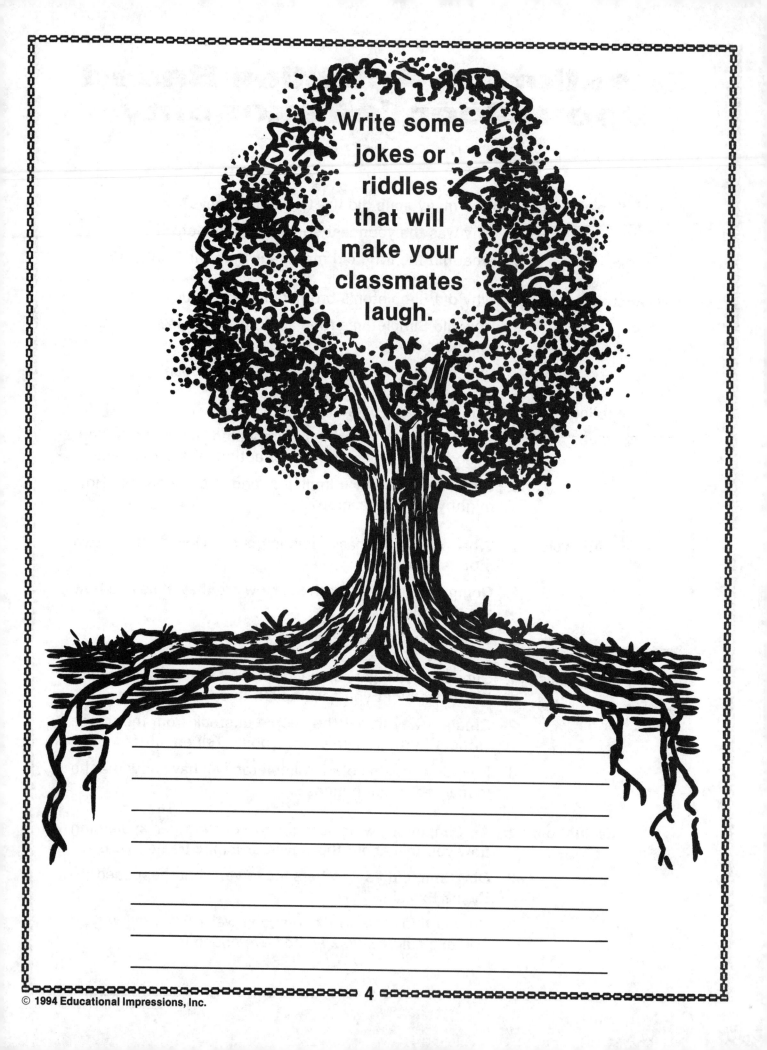

Write some jokes or riddles that will make your classmates laugh.

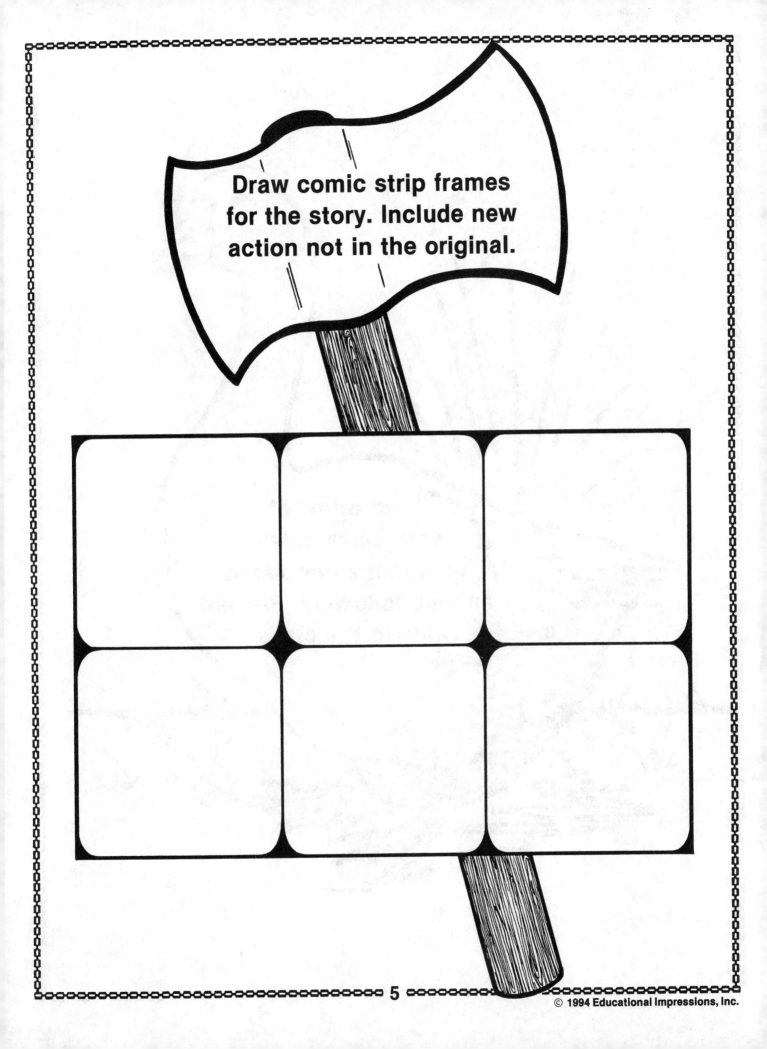

Draw comic strip frames for the story. Include new action not in the original.

5

With a few of
your classmates,
pantomine Simpleton
and his followers. Present
this to the class.

Write a different set of repeating actions for the little old man to use on the three brothers.

_____

_____

_____

_____

_____

_____

_____

_____

_____

_____

_____

_____

_____

Write another ending for the story.

Tell what happened to the golden goose.

_____

_____

_____

_____

_____

_____

_____

_____

_____

_____

_____

_____

_____

_____

_____

_____

Such Is the
Way of the
World

Such Is the Way of the World

by Benjamin Elkin

STORY SUMMARY

Set in Africa, this is the tale of Desta, a young boy who is given the responsibility of taking his father's cattle to the grasslands. He sets out with his pet monkey on his shoulder. But the monkey is frightened by a barking dog and runs away, startling the cows and causing them, too, to wander off.

As Desta searches for his monkey, he encounters many people. Each causes him to lose something, but each gives him something else in return saying, "Such is the way of the world."

The story ends happily with a hunter giving Desta a monkey in return for a spear he has broken. Desta is thrilled to find that the monkey is his own beloved lost pet. When he sees that the cattle are just ahead of him, he feels that all is right with the world!

Questions & Activities Based Upon Bloom's Taxonomy

Such Is the Way of the World

Knowledge:
1. What kind of pet did Desta have?
2. What did the dog's owner give to Desta?
3. How were Desta's ostrich feathers used?

Comprehension:
1. How did Desta's pot break?
2. What did the woman do to make up for the loss of Desta's feathers?
3. Explain how Desta went about trying to find his lost pet.

Application:
1. Have you ever lost a special pet? If so, how did you feel?
2. What is meant by the phrase "Such is the way of the world"?
3. This folk tale comes from Africa. Share with the class what you know about Africa.

Analysis:
1. Categorize the different things that were given to Desta.
2. Compare this folk tale to others you have read. How are they alike? How are they different?
3. Write three questions you would like to ask Desta about having a monkey as a pet.

Synthesis:
1. Suppose Desta had not found his pet. How would the story have been different?
2. Design a way Desta would never lose his pet again yet could still enjoy his company.
3. Create two other things given to and lost by Desta before he found his pet.

Evaluation:
1. Recommend this book to a friend. Give at least three reasons why your friend should read this book.
2. Could Desta have done something differently to protect his monkey? Explain.
3. Do you think that Desta was a generous person? Why or why not?

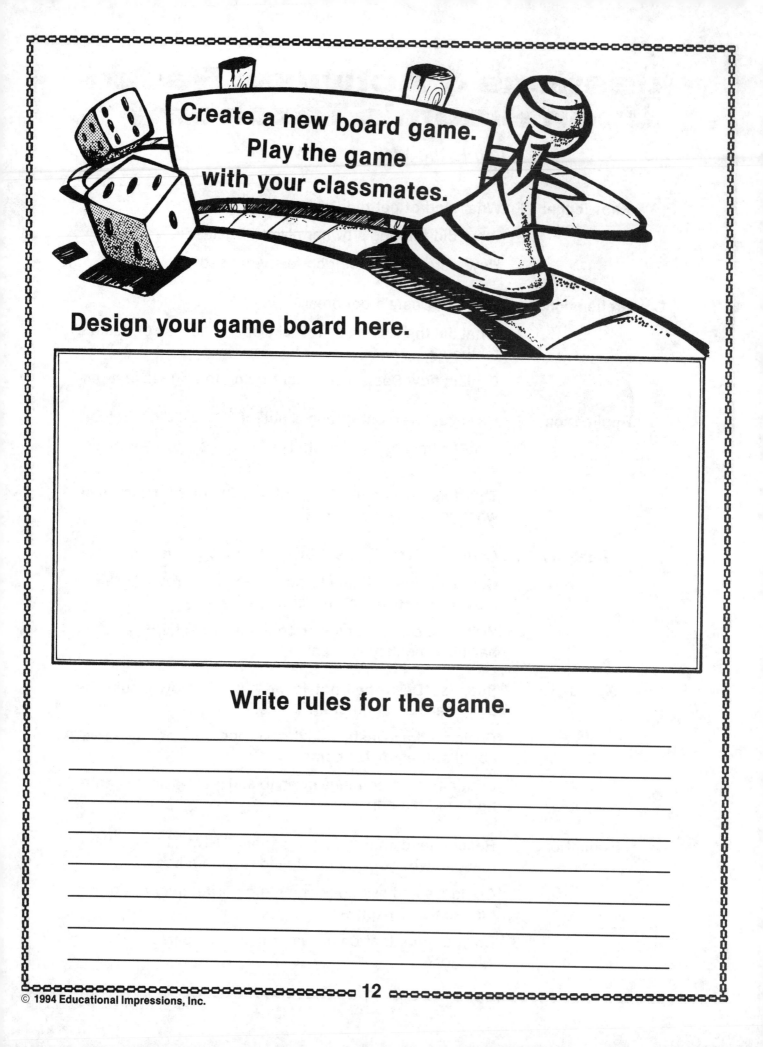

Create a new board game.
Play the game
with your classmates.

Design your game board here.

Write rules for the game.

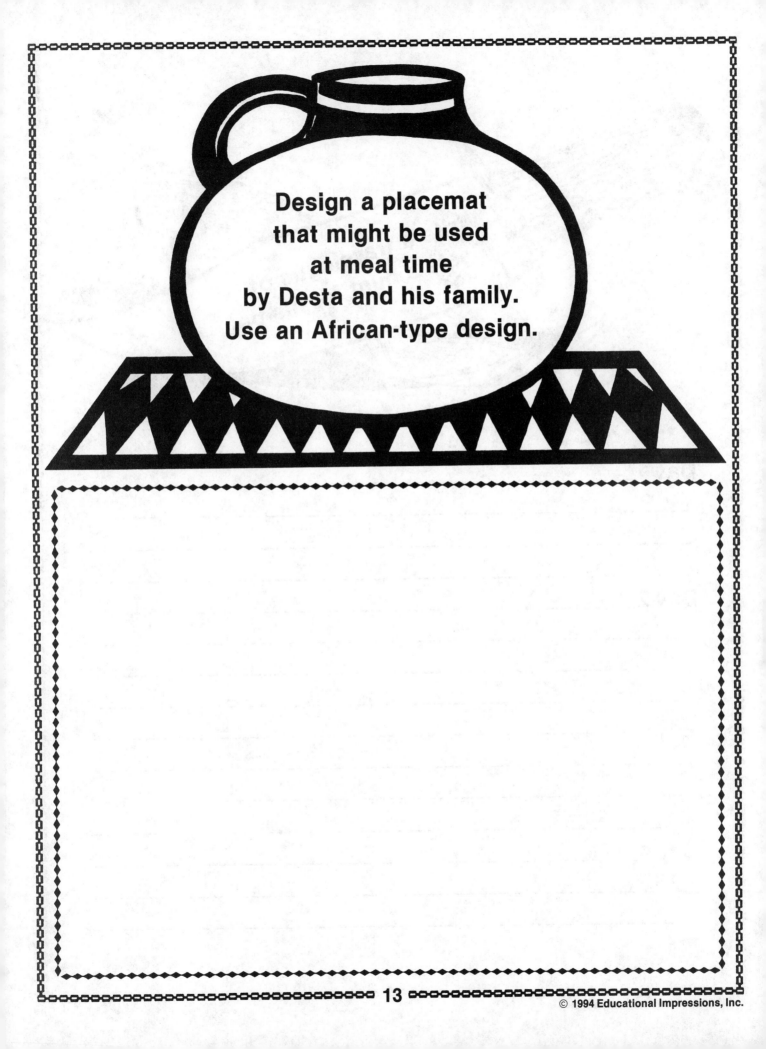

Design a placemat
that might be used
at meal time
by Desta and his family.
Use an African-type design.

13

Write a travelogue of
Desta's hunt for his pet.

Day 1_____
_____
_____
_____

Day 2_____
_____
_____
_____

Day 3_____
_____
_____
_____

Day 4_____
_____
_____

**Write a lost-and-found
ad for the newspaper that will
help Desta get back his monkey.**

_____

_____

_____

_____

_____

_____

_____

Be sure to include a picture of the monkey.

Write
about another way Desta might have found his pet.

_____

_____

_____

_____

_____

_____

_____

_____

_____

The Bremen Town Musicians

The Bremen Town Musicians

by the Brothers Grimm

STORY SUMMARY

Many years ago there was a donkey that had served his master well. The donkey grew old, and his master planned to do away with him. The donkey decided to leave and to make his way to Bremen to become a town musician.

As he walked along the road he met an old hunting dog. The dog had run away because he was too old and fat to do a good job of hunting. His master had planned to shoot him. The donkey explained what he was going to do and invited the dog to join him. The dog accepted and the two traveled down the road to Bremen.

Before long they met a cat. The cat explained that she had gotten too old and weak to chase mice and that her mistress planned to drown her. The donkey explained what he and the dog were going to do and asked the cat to join them. She did so happily.

At a farmyard down the road they met an old rooster on a gatepost. He was crowing very loudly. The rooster explained that his master had decided to make him into chicken soup and that this would be his last chance to crow. The donkey explained what he, the dog, and the cat were doing and he asked the rooster to join them. The rooster jumped at the chance to avoid becoming chicken soup!

When night arrived, the friends looked for a place to spend the night. They settled down in the middle of a forest. The rooster, who had jumped onto the branch of a tree, could see distant lights. He told the others that there must be a house ahead. The group decided to seek shelter in the house.

When they reached the lighted house, they peeked into a window and saw a table heaped with good things to eat. A band of robbers sat around the table enjoying the feast. The four friends came up with a plan to get rid of the robbers: They would all make their music so loudly that it would scare them away. The plan worked! The robbers ran away, and the animals went into the house to eat and sleep.

After midnight, however, the robbers came back. The house was dark and quiet. One of the robbers cautiously crept inside the house. He saw the cat's eyes glowing like smoldering embers. The robber tried to light a match for a closer look, and the cat jumped on him and scratched him. The dog then jumped up and bit his leg. Then the donkey kicked him sharply, and the rooster crowed loudly.

The frightened robber ran back to the band and told the others that a witch had scratched his face, a man had stabbed him in the leg, a monster attacked him with a club, and an old judge had ordered that they catch the crook. The band of robbers quickly ran away, never to return.

The four friends were so comfortable in their new home that they never did continue their journey to Bremen. They stayed and together made wonderful music under the stars.

Note: Ilse Plume's version of this tale was a Caldecott Honor Book.

Questions & Activities Based Upon Bloom's Taxonomy

The Bremen Town Musicians

Knowledge:
1. Why did the miller want to get rid of the donkey?
2. Where did the animals want to go? Why?
3. What was to become of the rooster?

Comprehension:
1. Explain some of the duties of a hunting dog.
2. Why did the animals choose to become musicians?
3. How did the animals find the house in the woods?

Application:
1. How would you go about becoming a musician?
2. What would you do if you met some robbers?
3. If you were a hunting dog too old to hunt, what would you do with the rest of your life?

Analysis:
1. Compare the animals' lives to your own life. How are they alike and how are they different?
2. Categorize the animals. Tell a little about each.
3. Repetition is common to most folk tales. Analyze the story and identify the repeated lines or actions.

Synthesis:
1. Add two or three animals to the group. Why did you choose those animals?
2. Create another way the animals might have gotten rid of the robbers.
3. Invent a home for homeless animals. Tell about it.

Evaluation:
1. Judge the owners' decisions to get rid of their animals.
2. If you had a pet, would you get rid of it just because it was old? Why or why not?
3. Was it right for the animals to take over the cabin? Why do you feel as you do?

Pretend you are a reporter. You have just interviewed the robber who was surprised by the animals. What questions did you ask him? How did he respond?

Reporter: _____

_____

Robber: _____

_____

Reporter: _____

_____

Robber: _____

_____

Reporter: _____

_____

Robber: _____

_____

Write a song that the Bremen Town Musicians might sing about themselves.

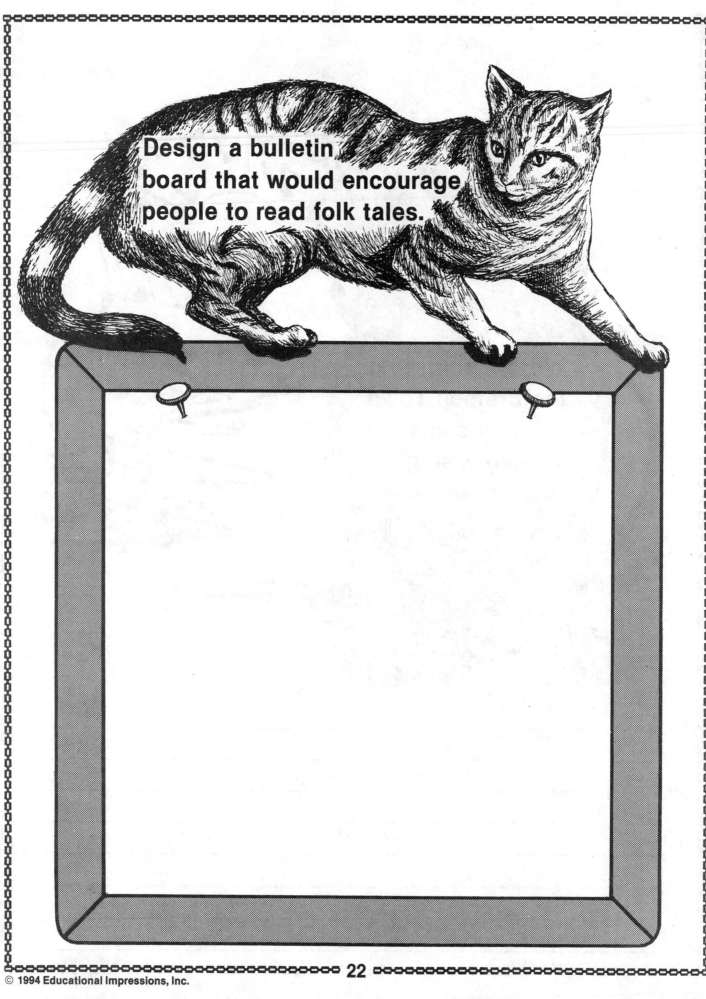

Design a bulletin board that would encourage people to read folk tales.

The Brothers Grimm are
responsible for many
folk tales. Research them.

Make copies of the fact file form. Use them to record your information. Share your findings with the class.

FACT FILE FORM

SUBJECT: _____

RESOURCE: _____

FACTS: _____

Write a sequel to this story.

Tell about the animals' lives in their new home.

_____

_____

_____

_____

_____

_____

_____

_____

_____

_____

_____

_____

_____

_____

_____

_____

24

Snow White
and
Rose Red

Snow White and Rose Red

by the Brothers Grimm

STORY SUMMARY

Once upon a time there was a widow who had two beautiful daughters named Snow White and Rose Red. Both girls were gentle and lovely.

One cold winter night a bear came to their home. He assured them that he meant them no harm and asked if he could spend the winter nights in their home. The kind widow said that he could.

Every night that winter the bear stayed in the warmth of the cottage. Every day he disappeared into the woods. Finally, spring came, and the forest was green once again. The bear told them that he must leave them so that he could protect his belongings from the evil dwarfs who would be out again now that it was spring. The girls were very sad, for they had grown very fond of their new friend.

One day as Snow White and Rose Red were gathering kindling, they heard a dwarf screaming that his beard was caught in a tree stump. The girls tried to untangle his beard, but they could not. Wanting to help him, Snow White took out her scissors and cut off the end of his beard. The dwarf complained about the loss of his beard and went off grumbling.

A short time later Snow White and Rose Red again encountered the dwarf. This time his beard was caught in a fishing line. Once again he begged for their help. Not knowing what else to do, Rose Red took out her scissors and cut off some more of the dwarf's beard. Again he screamed at the way they had disfigured him. He picked up his sack of pearls and stamped away.

A little while later the girls heard a pitiful cry as they walked to the village. A large bird was about to carry off the dwarf. The girls managed to pull the little man away from the bird. In typical fashion, the dwarf complained that they had torn his coat. He left with his sack of precious stones.

As they continued on, they saw the dwarf with his stones spread out on a rock. A great growl could be heard throughout the forest. It was their friend the bear. The bear swung his paw and sent the dwarf spinning, never to be seen again.

Suddenly, the bear's fur fell off, and a handsome prince stood before them. The dwarf had cast a spell on the prince and had stolen his treasure. The prince explained that only the dwarf's death could set him free.

Snow White and the prince were married. Rose Red married the prince's brother. They all lived happily ever after.

Questions & Activities Based Upon Bloom's Taxonomy

Snow White and Rose Red

Knowledge:
1. What did the sisters gather in the forest?
2. Who knocked at their door in the winter?
3. What did the bear seek?

Comprehension:
1. To what were the two daughters compared?
2. How did the girls stay busy in the winter?
3. What did Snow White really see when she thought she saw gold as the bear left?

Application:
1. How might you react if you opened your door and saw a bear standing there?
2. Demonstrate how the dwarf might have looked with his beard caught in the tree.
3. Repetition is a common characteristic of folk tales. Describe the repeating actions and lines in this story.

Analysis:
1. What three questions might you ask the prince about being a bear?
2. Dissect this or another folk tale you have read. Include main character(s), plan of events, repeated events, sayings or phrases, and real and imaginary elements.
3. Compare the personalities of the two girls and the dwarf.

Synthesis:
1. Devise another way the girls might have saved the dwarf from each predicament.
2. Imagine that you were one of the girls. Create a short skit that shows how you would have reacted to his rudeness.
3. Design a home for Snow White and the prince.

Evaluation:
1. Could this Snow White be the same Snow White as in *Snow White and the Seven Dwarfs?* Explain.
2. Judge whether the bear had the right to kill the dwarf.
3. As the prince, give reasons why you chose Snow White rather than Rose Red to be your wife.

Set up a story map for this story.

This is a story map for Jack and the Beanstalk.

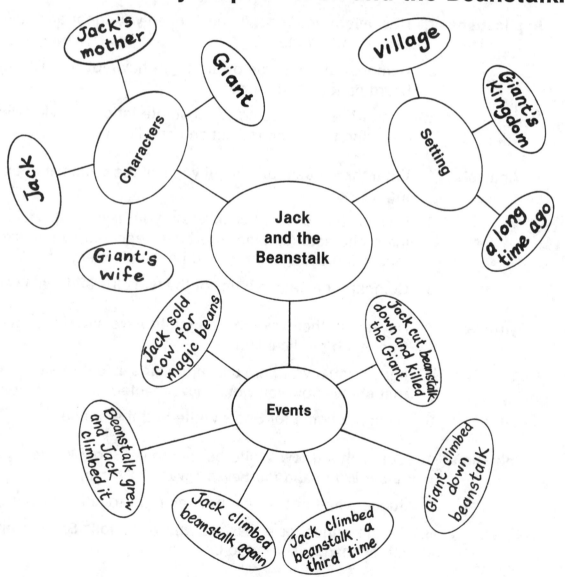

Plan a scavenger hunt
for your class.

**Decide on the prizes and where you will hide them.
Prepare a list of clues.**

Prizes	Where I Will Hide Them
1. _____	_____
2. _____	_____
3. _____	_____
4. _____	_____
5. _____	_____

Clues for Finding the Prizes:

1. _____

_____

2. _____

_____

3. _____

_____

4. _____

_____

5. _____

_____

29

**Find out more about bears.
Share what you learn with the class.**

**Make copies of the fact file form.
Use them to record your information.**

FACT FILE FORM

SUBJECT:

RESOURCE:

FACTS:

Pretend you are the dwarf. Draw a map to help you hide your treasures.

Tell why you chose each hiding place.

_____

_____

_____

_____

_____

_____

Write a sequel to this story.

Tell about Snow White's and Rose Red's lives after they each marry a prince.

_____

_____

_____

_____

_____

_____

_____

_____

_____

_____

_____

_____

_____

_____

_____

_____

The Funny Little Woman

The Funny Little Woman

by Lafcadio Hearn

retold by Arlene Mosel

STORY SUMMARY

This is the story of a funny little woman who lived many years ago in Japan. Everything struck her funny, and she always laughed the same funny little laugh.

The funny little woman loved to make dumplings from rice. One day one of her dumplings rolled off her table and down a hole in the floor to a place where the terrible *oni* lived. Although warned to stay clear of the *oni* by the statues of gods along the road, the little woman did not heed their advice. When she heard one of the *oni* say that he smelled a human, she could not help but laugh. The *oni* captured her and took her back to his village to make rice dumplings for him and the other *oni*.

At first she was content to make rice dumplings for them, but eventually she began to miss her home. After an exciting adventure, the funny little woman managed to escape. She took with her a magic paddle that the *oni* had given her. With it she could make a whole pot of rice with just one grain. The funny little woman was able to make and sell many dumplings and she lived happily ever after.

Questions & Activities Based Upon Bloom's Taxonomy

The Funny Little Woman

Knowledge:
1. What skill did the funny little woman have that caused the *oni* to want her?
2. Where does this story take place?
3. What is another word for *oni*?

Comprehension:
1. What was so special about the magic paddle?
2. Explain the statues' warning.
3. What caused the woman to be caught by the *oni*?

Application:
1. Explain the definition of a statue.
2. What special things does your mother or father cook?
3. If you were interviewing the *oni,* what questions would you ask about the funny little woman's cooking?

Analysis:
1. What are some of the *oni's* good and bad characteristics? (Find at least one good quality.)
2. What might have caused the ground to cave in around the funny little woman?
3. Think of some other ways the funny little woman might have made her fortune.

Synthesis:
1. Create a new ending in which the little woman does not escape from the *oni.*
2. Propose another way the funny little woman might have escaped.
3. Create another talent the funny little woman might have shared with the *oni.*

Evaluation:
1. If you had as great a fortune as the funny little woman, how would you spend your money? Give reasons to support your spending.
2. How will the *oni* eat now that the funny little woman is gone? Why do you think this?
3. Judge whether or not it was right for the little woman to take the magic paddle. Explain.

Create an underground world of your own.

Draw a picture of your underground world.

Describe your underground world. Where is it? Who lives there and what do they do? What is life like?

_____

_____

_____

_____

_____

_____

_____

Using a shoebox and art supplies, make a diorama of the oni's underground world.

Supply List

pompom balls
shoebox
paint and brush
colored pencils
glue
markers
cotton balls
rocks
dirt
glitter
papier-mache
drinking straws

beans
chalk
clay
play doh
scissors
pencils
crayons
sticks
sequins
foam
balloons
newspaper

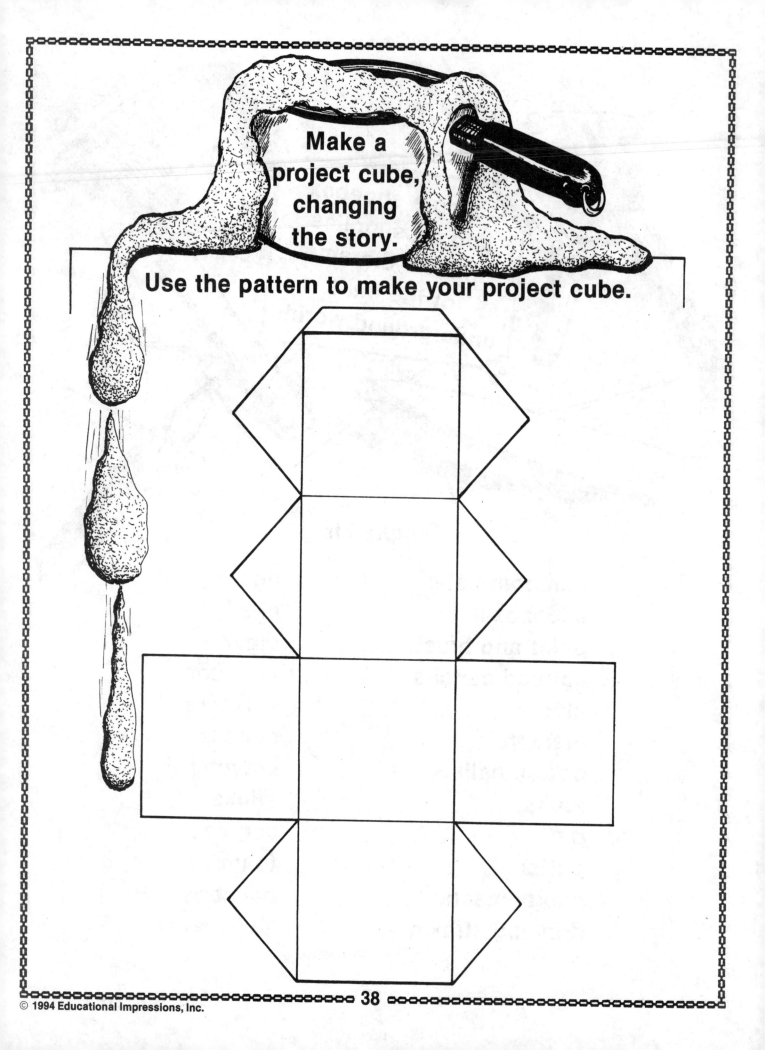

Make a project cube, changing the story.

Use the pattern to make your project cube.

Pretend to be
the funny woman.
Write a letter to
the oni. Express your
feelings about being
forced to be their cook.

Dear oni,

Write a continuation of this story.

Tell how the funny little woman's life changes as a result of her fortune.

_____

_____

_____

_____

_____

_____

_____

_____

_____

_____

_____

_____

_____

_____

_____

_____

_____

_____

Stone Soup

Stone Soup

by Marcia Brown

STORY SUMMARY

Many years ago three soldiers were traveling home from the war. They were tired and hungry and wanted a place to spend the night. The soldiers saw a village ahead of them. They hoped to be given some food to eat and a place to sleep. But the villagers saw them coming and hid all their food.

The soldiers went to each house and asked for food; each time they were told that none could be spared. The soldiers then decided that they would have to make stone soup. The villagers had never heard of stone soup and were very curious.

The soldiers asked the villagers to bring them a pot, fire, some water, and three smooth stones. One by one, the soldiers suggested other ingredients to enhance the soup: salt and pepper, carrots, cabbage, potatoes, meat, barley, and milk. The villagers gladly provided them.

Before long, the soldiers had a huge pot of boiling stone soup. The villagers set up tables and brought out roasts and bread. There was feasting, singing, and dancing!

When everyone was full, the soldiers asked if there was a hay loft where they might sleep. Instead, they were offered shelter in the finest homes. After a good night's sleep, the soldiers went on their way, and the villagers thanked them for showing them how to make stone soup.

Note: This Caldecott Honor Book was based upon an old English folk tale. There are other versions. You might want to have the class read another version and compare the two.

Questions & Activities Based Upon Bloom's Taxonomy

Stone Soup

Knowledge:
1. How many soldiers were in this story?
2. Where did the peasants hide the barley?
3. What ingredients did the soldiers ask for?

Comprehension:
1. Why did the peasants hide the food?
2. In what country does this version of the story take place? What makes you think that?
3. Describe how the soup was made. Were the stones really necessary? Explain.

Application:
1. What kind of soup is your favorite? If you have ever helped make soup, tell what you did to help.
2. How might you react if some soldiers came to your house asking for food?
3. If you were one of the villagers, what excuse would you give for not sharing your food?

Analysis:
1. Find a recipe for soup in a cook book. Compare it to the way the soldiers made soup. How are they alike and how are they different?
2. Why did the soldiers suggest that they make stone soup?
3. What kind of men do you think the soldiers were? Why do you think this?

Synthesis:
1. Predict what might have happened if the soldiers had tried to force the villagers into sharing their food.
2. Pretend that you are the mayor. What might you do to make the soldiers comfortable in your home?
3. Suppose the peasants had not been fooled by the soldiers' plan. Create a new ending for the story.

Evaluation:
1. What valuable lesson can be learned from this tale?
2. Do you think the villagers were selfish? Why or why not?
3. Give a few reasons why you did or did not enjoy this story.

Write a recipe for stone soup.

STONE SOUP

Ingredients:

_____
_____
_____
_____
_____
_____

Directions:

_____
_____
_____
_____
_____
_____
_____
_____
_____

44

Design an ad
for stone soup.

Create a mobile with a folk tale theme.

Plan your design here...

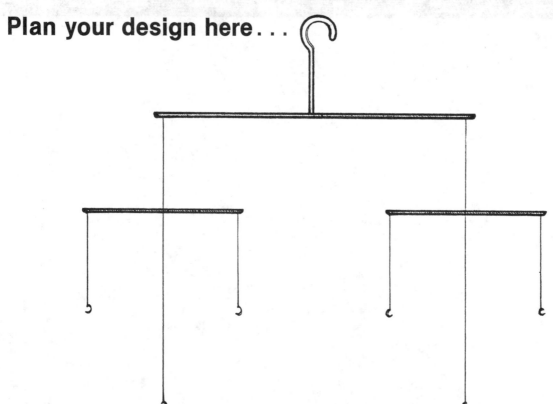

Formulate
a new plan to
trick the villagers
into sharing
their food.

List all of your ideas. Put a check next to your best idea.

_____

_____

_____

_____

_____

_____

_____

_____

_____

_____

_____

47

Write about the soldiers' lives after they left the village.

Begin with their conversation as they walked away from the village.

_____

_____

_____

_____

_____

_____

_____

_____

_____

_____

_____

_____

_____

_____

_____

_____

Ming Lo
Moves
The Mountain

Ming Lo Moves the Mountain

by Arnold Lobel

STORY SUMMARY

This is the story of Ming Lo and his wife. They lived at the bottom of a large mountain in a nice little house. Although they loved their home, they did not like living so close to the mountain. Ming Lo's wife begged him to move the mountain.

Ming Lo asked the village wise man for advise, and the wise man suggested several things that he might try. Ming Lo did as he was told, but the mountain did not move. Finally, the wise man suggested that they take down their house and bind it together. He then told them to take their house and their belongings with them as they did a special dance. He told them to keep their eyes closed while putting one foot behind the other. The dance, he said, would take several hours.

Ming Lo and his wife followed the wise man's directions very carefully. When the dance was over and they opened their eyes, the mountain had moved! They rebuilt their house and were very happy.

Questions & Activities Based Upon Bloom's Taxonomy

Ming Lo Moves the Mountain

Knowledge:
1. What was wrong with their roof?
2. Where did the wise man live?
3. What did Ming Lo and his wife drop from the top of the mountain?

Comprehension:
1. Why didn't Ming Lo and his wife love the mountain?
2. Why wouldn't Ming Lo's garden grow well?
3. Chart the ways the wise man advised Ming Lo to move the mountain.

Application:
1. How would you move a mountain?
2. What advice would you have given to Ming Lo?
3. Write directions for a game. Make them clear so that someone who has never played will understand what to do.

Analysis:
1. Why did the wise man give Ming Lo such silly tasks?
2. If you were the wise man, how would you feel about Ming Lo after telling him these ways to move the mountain?
3. What qualities must a person have to be classified as wise?

Synthesis:
1. Create another way the wise man could have had Ming Lo move the mountain.
2. As a reporter, interview the wise man. Prepare three questions to ask him about his advice on moving the mountain. How might the wise man answer your questions?
3. Devise a way to get to the top of the mountain without climbing it.

Evaluation:
1. What was wrong with the wise man's advice to Ming Lo about moving the mountain?
2. If you could move anywhere in the world, where would you move? Why?
3. Do you think Ming Lo and his wife will be happy in their new location? Why or why not?

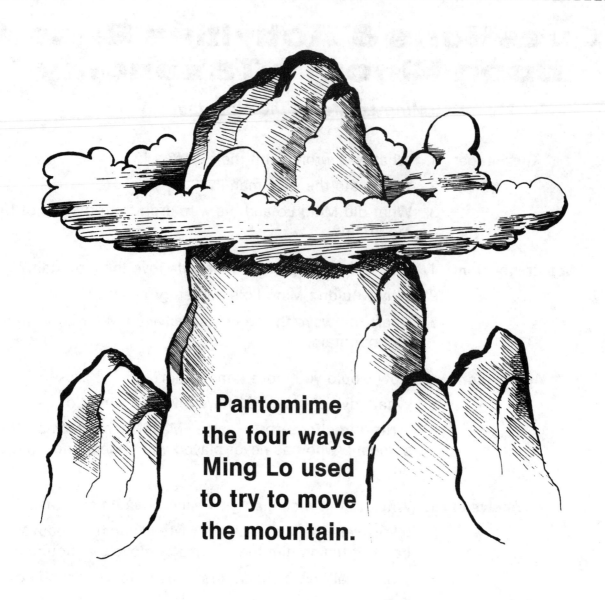

Pantomime the four ways Ming Lo used to try to move the mountain.

List the ways here . . .

_____

_____

_____

_____

_____

_____

_____

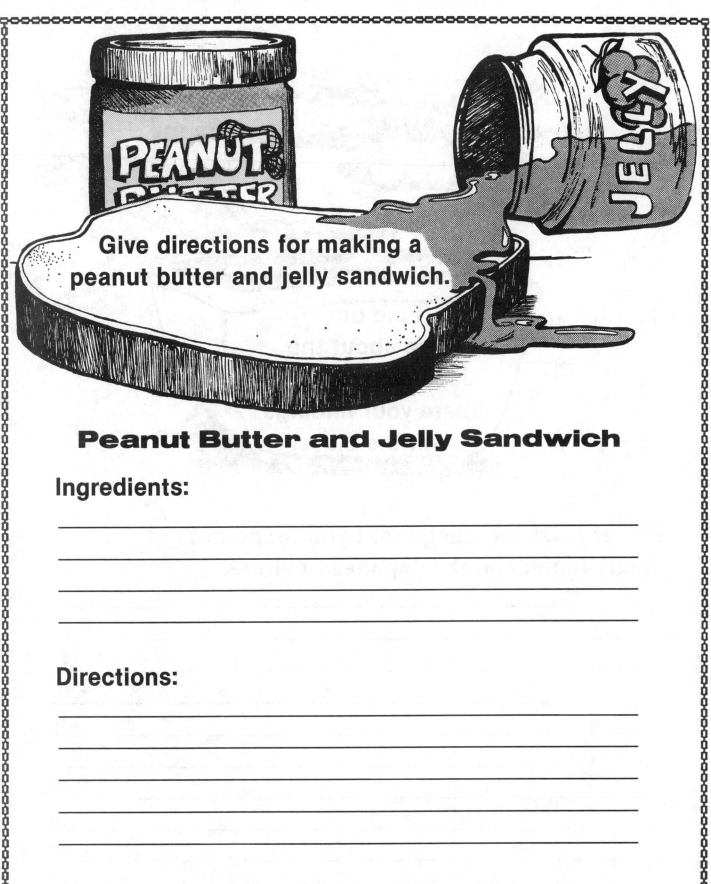

Give directions for making a peanut butter and jelly sandwich.

Peanut Butter and Jelly Sandwich

Ingredients:

_____
_____
_____
_____

Directions:

_____
_____
_____
_____
_____

See if a younger child can make a peanut butter and jelly sandwich by following your directions.

Find out more about the Japanese culture. Share your findings with the class.

List at least ten things that you found out about Japan and the Japanese culture.

_____

_____

_____

_____

_____

_____

_____

_____

_____

_____

Create an impossible task for someone to do. Give that task to your classmates to see how they would suggest solving the problem.

Write

a paragraph to Ming Lo and his wife about what has just happened.

Explain to them that it was they and their house that moved and not the mountain. Be convincing!

The Three
Little
Pigs

The Three Little Pigs

retold by Joseph Jacobs

STORY SUMMARY

This old English tale tells the story of a mother pig and her three sons. They lived long ago in a nice little house until the day came that the three pigs had to leave and live their own lives.

The first little pig met a man with some straw. He asked the man to give him some to build a house. The man did, and in no time, the first little pig had built a house of straw.

The second little pig met a man with some sticks. He asked the man for some sticks so he could build a house. The man did, and in no time, the second little pig had built a house of sticks.

The third little pig wanted something that would withstand the weather and protect him from dangerous animals. He got some bricks from the brick man. Building a house of bricks was a lot harder and took a lot more work than building one of straw or sticks, but the third little pig thought the extra effort was worth it. Eventually, he finished building his house of bricks.

Meanwhile, a wolf visited the straw house of the first little pig. He told him to let him in or he would huff and puff and blow his house down. The pig answered, "Not by the hair of my chinny chin chin." But the wolf huffed and puffed and blew the house down and he ate the first little pig. The hungry wolf then went to the stick house of the second little pig. The second little pig suffered the same fate as the first.

When the wolf saw the brick house of the third pig, he knew it would not be easy to blow it down. He decided to trick the pig. He told the pig about a wonderful turnip patch and arranged to meet him there. The pig outsmarted him, however, and went to the turnip patch early, returning home before the wolf got there. The wolf then told the pig about an apple tree with delicious apples. Again the pig got there early and returned home before the wolf arrived. Finally, the wolf told him about a wonderful fair, thinking he would fool the pig and get there early to catch him. But the pig was too smart and went to the fair even earlier than the wolf.

By this time the wolf had grown very angry. He climbed up onto the roof of the brick house and came down the chimney. But the third little pig was too clever for him. He guessed what the wolf would do and he was ready for him. The wolf fell into a pot of boiling water, and that was the end of the mean old wolf!

Note: There are several versions of this folk tale. You might want the children to read more than one and compare them.

Questions & Activities Based Upon Bloom's Taxonomy

The Three Little Pigs

Knowledge:
1. Who decided it was time for the pigs to leave home?
2. Name the materials used by each to build his house.
3. Who visited each little pig?

Comprehension:
1. Recite the wolf's famous line.
2. Recite the pigs' famous response.
3. Why couldn't the wolf eat the third little pig?

Application:
1. List the materials you might need to build a house.
2. If you were the wolf, what would you have offered the pig to get him out of the house?
3. Because of his greed, the wolf eventually destroyed himself. Have you ever known a greedy person? If so, tell about that person.

Analysis:
1. How might the first two pigs have saved themselves from the wolf?
2. Develop three questions to ask the wolf about his eating habits.
3. Make a story diagram of this folk tale. Show the plot, setting, action, and climax.

Synthesis:
1. Suppose the third pig had built his house of wood. How might the story have been different?
2. Devise a different way for the third pig to solve his problem with the wolf.
3. Predict how the third pig's experience with the wolf will affect his future.

Evaluation:
1. Which pig was the smartest. Why?
2. There are several different versions of this folk tale. Read at least one other. Which do you like best? Why?
3. If you were the mother pig, how might you feel about your sons' misfortune? Would you feel guilty? Why or why not?

Organize
a way to trap
the wolf.

Describe your plan.

_____

_____

_____

_____

_____

What roles will your classmates, teacher, and/or relatives play in carrying out your plan?

_____

_____

_____

_____

_____

_____

_____

_____

_____

Retell the story from the wolf's point of view!

Write your story here.

_____

_____

_____

_____

_____

_____

_____

_____

If you wish, record your story.

Using art materials, build a model of a house that could escape the wolf's huffing and puffing.

Supply List

pompom balls	beans
shoebox	chalk
paint and brush	clay
colored pencils	play doh
glue	scissors
markers	pencils
cotton balls	crayons
rocks	sticks
dirt	sequins
glitter	foam
papier-mache	balloons
drinking straws	newspaper

Design a wanted poster to help the law catch the mean old wolf.

Be sure to include a picture of the wolf.

Wanted: Dead or Alive

Write
a new and different ending for the story.

_____

_____

_____

_____

_____

_____

_____

_____

_____

_____

_____

_____

_____

_____

_____

Caps
for
Sale

Caps for Sale

by Esphyr Slobodkina

STORY SUMMARY

This is the story of a peddler who sold caps and carried his wares on top of his head. One day he settled under a large tree to take a nap. When he awoke, all the caps but his own were gone.

The peddler looked up and saw several monkeys in the tree. Each donned one of his caps. He tried to get them to throw down his caps. The peddler shook his finger and then his hands. He stomped one foot; then he stomped both. The monkeys merely mimicked what he did.

Finally, the peddler got so angry that he threw his own cap on the ground. To his surprise, the monkeys copied him and threw theirs on the ground too! The peddler gathered his wares and continued his journey calling, "Caps! Caps for Sale! Fifty cents a cap!"

Note: Although this is an original, modern tale, it is written in the traditional folk-tale style, with the rhythm and repetition typical of the old tales.

Questions & Activities Based Upon Bloom's Taxonomy

Caps for Sale

Knowledge:
1. What were the colors of the caps sold by the peddler?
2. How much did each cap cost?
3. What did the peddler do after he got back his caps?

Comprehension:
1. What caused the monkeys to return the caps?
2. List the different actions the peddler took to try to get back his caps.
3. Why didn't the peddler have money for lunch?

Application:
1. Retell the story, acting it out as you tell it.
2. Suppose you wanted to earn extra money. What might you sell? Why did you choose that?
3. How might you have helped the peddler sell his caps?

Analysis:
1. Where might the monkeys have come from?
2. Explain the popular phrase "monkey see, monkey do." How does this phrase relate to the story?
3. Find out what *monkeyshine* means. How does this relate to the story?

Synthesis:
1. Write an ending for this story in which the peddler has sold all of his caps. What will he do with the money?
2. How might the peddler make use of the monkeys?
3. What might have caused the monkeys to take the peddler's caps?

Evaluation:
1. Suppose you found something that didn't belong to you? What would you do?
2. Did you learn anything from this tale? What?
3. Do you feel that the peddler was successful at his job? Why or why not?

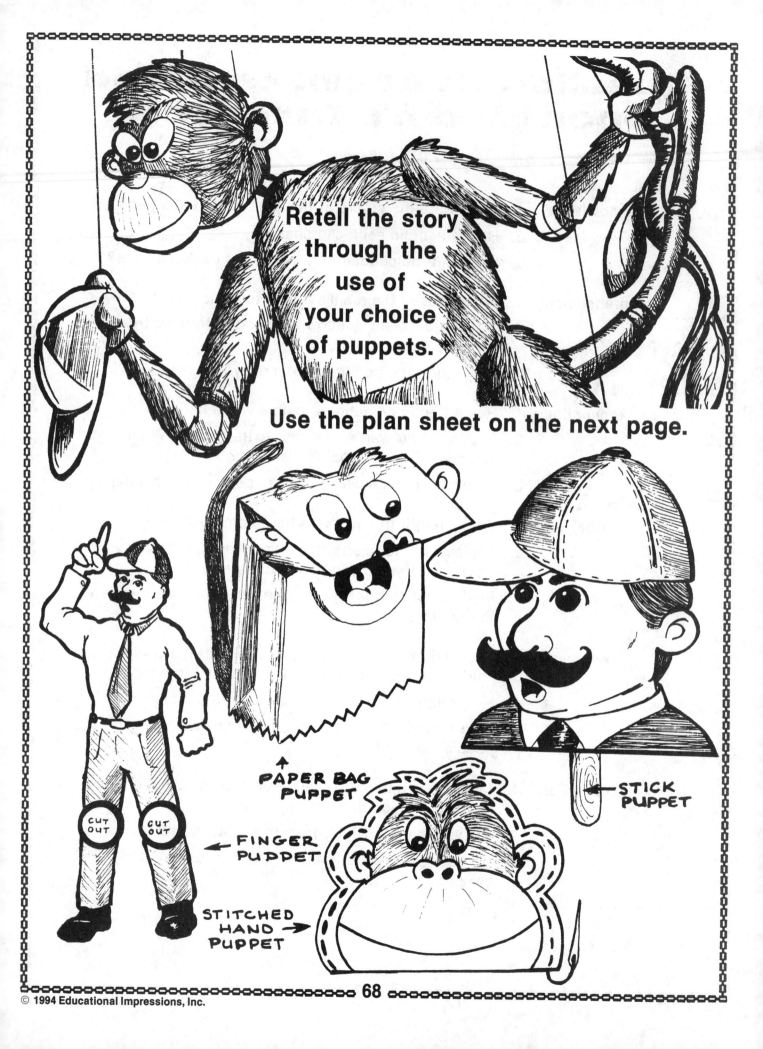

Retell the story through the use of your choice of puppets.

Use the plan sheet on the next page.

PAPER BAG PUPPET

STICK PUPPET

CUT OUT CUT OUT

FINGER PUPPET

STITCHED HAND PUPPET

PLAN SHEET

PROJECT _____

SUPPLIES NEEDED _____

_____

_____

_____

STEPS TO COMPLETE PROJECT _____

_____

_____

_____

_____

_____

WHAT PROBLEMS DID YOU HAVE? _____

_____

_____

_____

HOW COULD YOU HAVE MADE THE PROJECT BETTER? _____

_____

_____

_____

_____

69

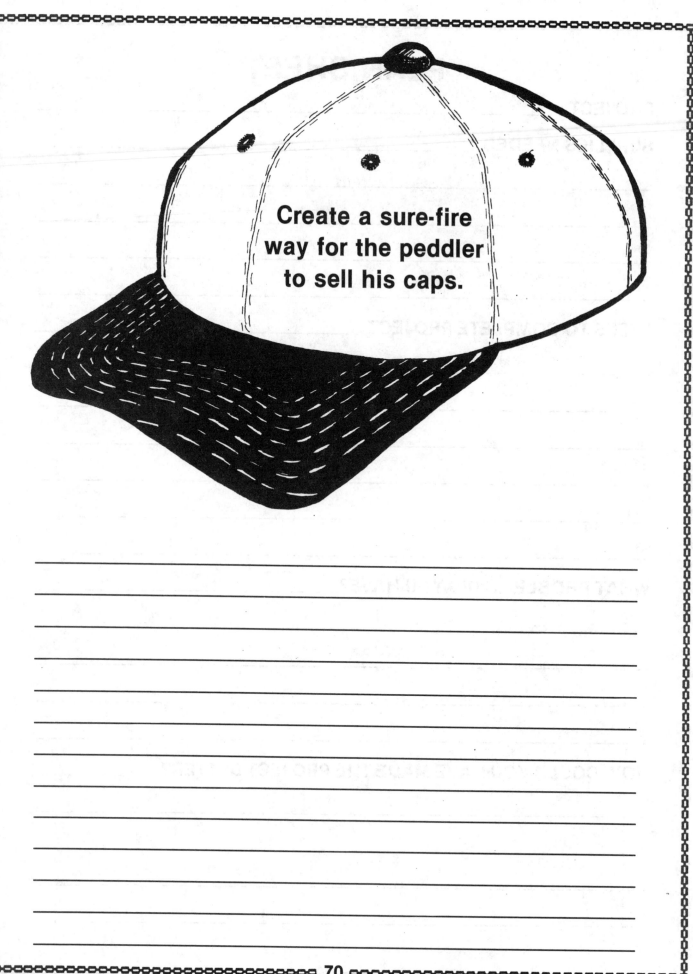

Create a sure-fire way for the peddler to sell his caps.

_____
_____
_____
_____
_____
_____
_____
_____
_____
_____
_____
_____

Research the
history of hats.
Share what you
learn with the class.

**Make copies of the fact file form.
Use them to record your information.**

	FACT FILE FORM	
	SUBJECT:	
◯	RESOURCE:	
	FACTS:	

Devise another way for
the peddler to carry his caps.

List your ideas here...

_____

_____

_____

_____

_____

_____

_____

_____

Put a ✔ next to the idea you like best.

Create a newspaper or TV ad to help the peddler sell his caps.

Write a brief biography of the peddler.

Include answers to these and other questions: Where does he live? Does he have a family? Does he have any pets? Who are his friends? Where does he get his caps? What else does he like to do?

_____

_____

_____

_____

_____

_____

_____

_____

_____

_____

_____

_____

_____

_____

_____

The Emperor's New Clothes

The Emperor's New Clothes

by Hans Christian Andersen

STORY SUMMARY

Many years ago an emperor lived in a far-away land. He loved new clothes and spent most of his money on them. One day two men came to the emperor. They said that they were weavers and that they could weave the emperor the most beautiful cloth in the world.

However, the men were not really weavers, but crooks. They convinced the emperor that their cloth was so fine that not everyone could see it; those who were stupid or not good at their job could not. The emperor thought this truly amazing and told them to weave the cloth for him. He paid them much gold and gave them the best silk thread in his kingdom.

The men pretended to work hard at the loom. Finally, the king sent his chief minister to see how the cloth was progressing. The minister could not see anything, but he was afraid to admit this to the king. He knew the king would think him stupid and not good at his job; therefore, the minister lied to the king and told him how beautiful the cloth was.

The next day the two men asked the king for more money and more thread. The emperor gave them what they wanted and a few days later sent his second chief minister to check on the cloth. He, too, was unable to see the cloth, but he didn't want the emperor to think him stupid and not good at his job, so he lied. He told the emperor how beautiful it was.

The emperor could wait no longer and went to see the weavers himself. He was surprised when he could not see the cloth, but he knew that he was not stupid and pretended that he thought the cloth was beautiful.

The two men then pretended to cut the cloth and to sew it into a new suit for the emperor. They lit candles throughout the night so that everyone would see how hard they were working. The next day the men went to the emperor and told him that they had brought with them his new suit. The emperor tried it on and said that his new clothes were as light as a feather.

The emperor was ready to parade in front of his people to show off his new suit. Two noblemen were asked to hold the corners of his new cape. They couldn't see it, but they pretended to hold up the ends anyway. The emperor began his parade in front of his people.

Everyone was anxious to see the emperor in his new clothes. They shouted that his clothes were beautiful even though no one could see them. Suddenly, a small child shouted, "He hasn't got anything on!" Soon everyone in the crowd was whispering, "The emperor hasn't got anything on!"

The emperor knew that his people were right, but he continued to walk proudly with his head held high. The two noblemen continued to walk behind him, holding the ends of the cape that wasn't really there.

Questions & Activities Based Upon Bloom's Taxonomy

The Emperor's New Clothes

Knowledge:
1. What did the emperor love best?
2. What did the two men pretend to be?
3. What did the men say was unique about their cloth?

Comprehension:
1. Why did the emperor's ministers tell him that the cloth was beautiful?
2. How did the emperor pay the men for their weaving?
3. Why did the weavers burn candles all night?

Application:
1. What would you have said if the emperor had asked you about the cloth?
2. Have you ever tricked someone or been tricked by someone? Tell about it.
3. What real-life problem could be solved by learning a lesson from this story?

Analysis:
1. Why did it take a child to expose the trick?
2. Compare the lesson learned from this tale to one learned in another. How are they alike and how are they different?
3. What questions might you ask the men about their weaving?

Synthesis:
1. Design a suit for the emperor that can be seen. Draw a picture of it.
2. Predict what would happen to the men if the emperor caught them.
3. Devise a way of testing the cloth that would convince the emperor that it wasn't really there.

Evaluation:
1. How do you think the emperor felt when he realized that he had been tricked?
2. Make a list of adjectives that could describe the emperor. Use them to write a brief character sketch of the emperor.
3. Decide who was more foolish, the emperor or his people. Tell why you feel as you do.

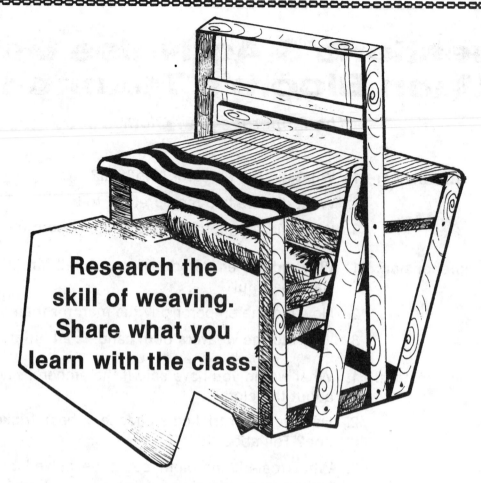

Research the skill of weaving. Share what you learn with the class.

Make copies of the fact file form.
Use them to record your information.

FACT FILE FORM

SUBJECT:

RESOURCE:

FACTS:

78

Demonstrate to the class how to use a needle and thread to sew material together.

Write down the steps you will follow.

_____

_____

_____

_____

_____

_____

_____

_____

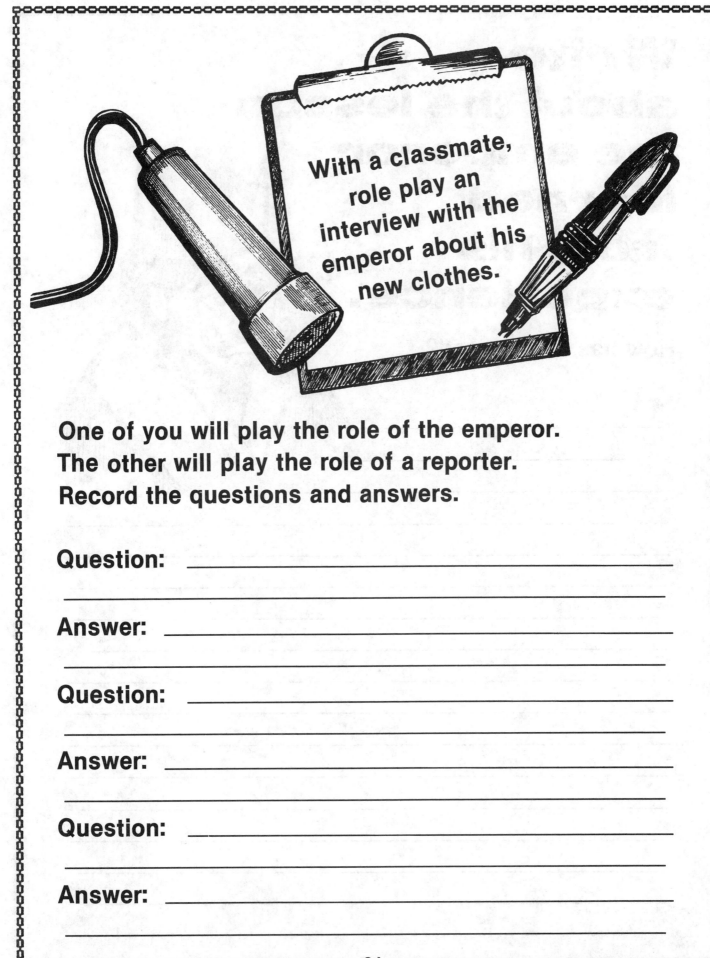

With a classmate, role play an interview with the emperor about his new clothes.

One of you will play the role of the emperor.
The other will play the role of a reporter.
Record the questions and answers.

Question: _____

_____

Answer: _____

_____

Question: _____

_____

Answer: _____

_____

Question: _____

_____

Answer: _____

_____

Write
about the lesson the emperor learned from his experience.

How has he changed?

_____

_____

_____

_____

_____

_____

_____

_____

_____

_____

_____

_____

_____

_____

_____

_____

Organizational Sheet for Writing a Folk Tale

Main Character:

_____

Other Characters:

_____   _____

_____   _____

_____   _____

Main Events:

_____

_____

_____

Other Events:

_____

_____

_____

Setting:

_____

Repeated Events, Sayings, and Phrases:

_____

_____

_____

Real and Make-believe Elements:

_____

_____

From Mean to Kind

Help change the big bad wolf from mean to kind by changing one letter at a time. The word clues on the left will help. The picture clues on this page will help too.

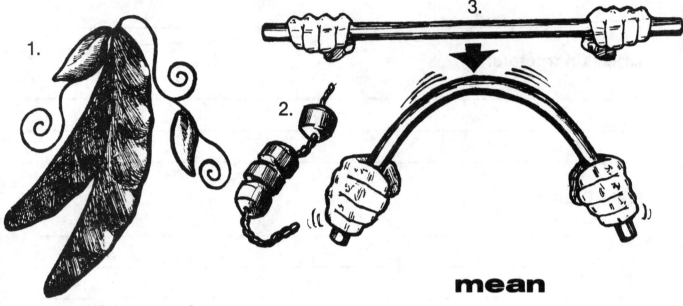

1. edible seed
2. can be strung
3. to curve
4. group of musicians
5. magician's stick
6. air that moves

mean

_____
_____
_____
_____
_____
_____

kind

From Prince to ?

The evil dwarf has turned the prince into an animal. Connect the dots in the correct order to find out what kind of animal the prince has become.

85

Folk-tale Word Search

Find the words and names listed below. You may look up, down, across, backwards or diagonally! Circle the words as you find them. One has been done for you. Have fun!

```
K R G K L M I N G L O U O C V P P R
Q I O H S I M P L E T O N A G S F W
T X O Y U E Z V F W A X B P Y C L D
Z E S F A D G B C C H B D S E A O F
G M E J S D E R E S O R D E R I W J
Y P V S N O W W H I T E N O S O P P
E E U T R S L Q S R T R U S V G Q W
K R U O D V O D W A R F Z W P X I A
N O Z N C E A N I D B M E C F D G P
O R J I E I S K F E J L G M K N H L
D P G I Q H J T R T R E A S U R E S
T L U M E V N F A W O S X P Y Q Z R
```

Caps	Goose	Simpleton
Desta	Ming Lo	Snow White
Donkey	Oni	Soldiers
Dwarf	Pigs	Treasure
Emperor	Rose Red	Wolf ✓

86

© 1994 Educational Impressions, Inc.

Folk-Tale Newsletter

Write a newsletter giving bits of news about characters from folk tales you have read. Your newsletter has been started for you with news about Jack's cutting down of the beanstalk.

FOLK-TALE NEWS

Giant Destroyed

The terrible giant was found dead today thanks to Jack, who chopped down the famous beanstalk.

_____
_____
_____
_____
_____
_____

_____ _____
_____ _____
_____ _____
_____ _____
_____ _____
_____ _____

Folk Tale Magic Game

DIRECTIONS

1. Copy or remove the gameboard sheets on pages 89 through 92. Mount them on heavy board.

2. Copy or remove page 103, which has pictures of the characters. Cut out the pictures and the stands and mount them on heavy board.

3. Copy or remove pages 93-102 and cut out the Question and Chance Cards.

4. Have each player choose a character. Two to six players (or teams of players) can play.

5. In clockwise fashion, each player draws a question card. If the player answers the question correctly, he/she moves ahead the number of spaces indicated on the card.

6. If the player lands on Chance, he/she draws a chance card. The player will move forward or backward as indicated on the card.

7. The first player to get back around to Start wins the game.

Note: These pages have been perforated for ease in removal; however, you may prefer to make copies of these pages and to keep the pages in the book for future reference.

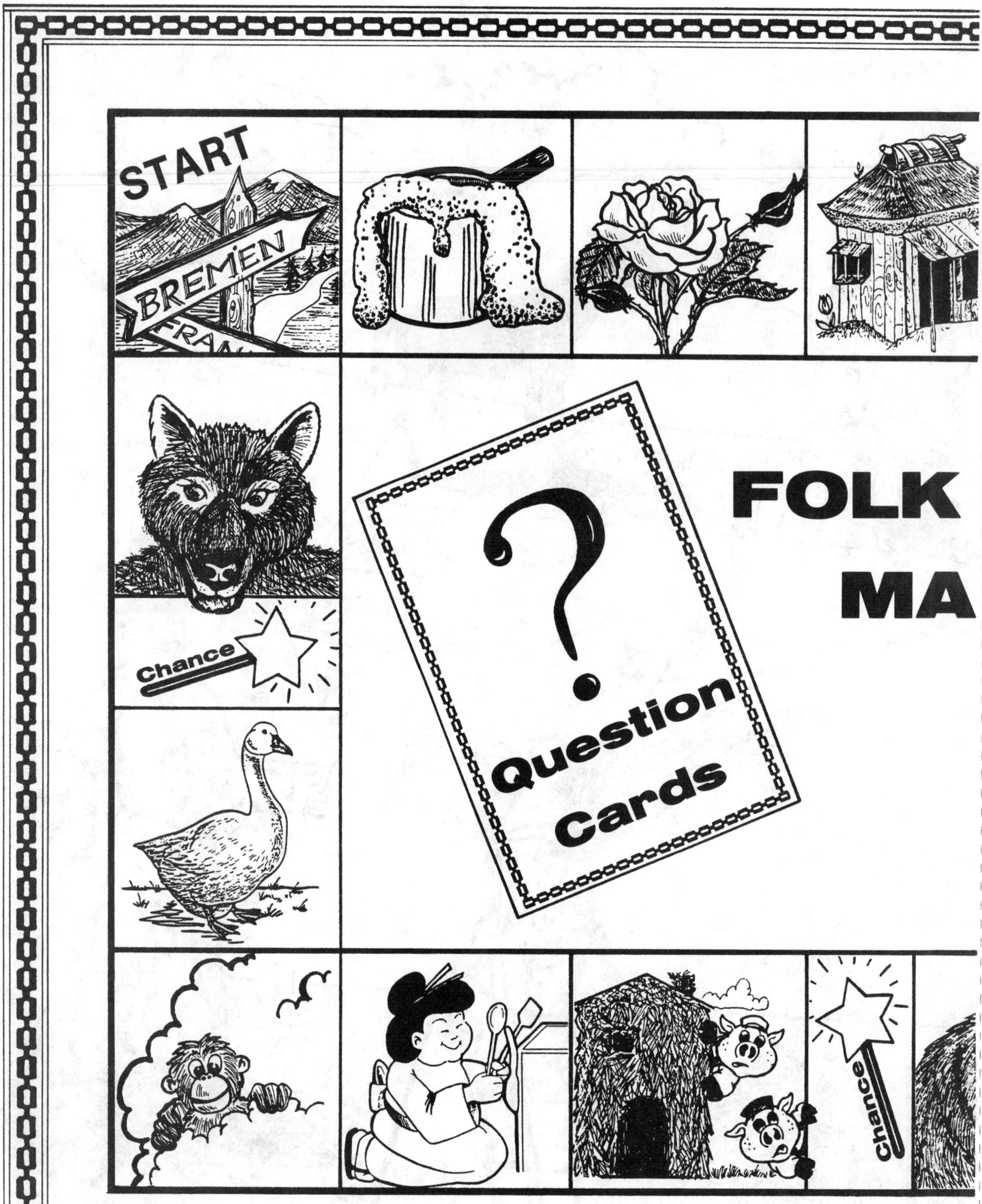
START
BREMEN
FRAN
FOLK
MA
Question
Cards
Chance
Chance

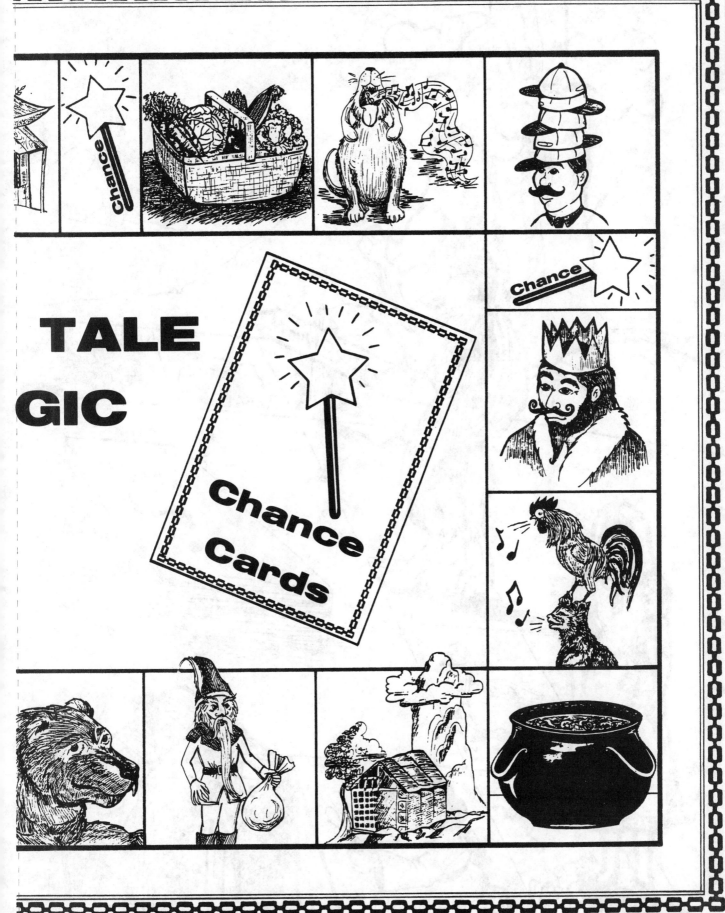

TALE
GIC

Chance
Cards

Describe the type of countryside around Simpleton's home.

(Move 2 spaces.)

Who captured the Funny Little Woman?

(Move 3 spaces.)

If you were the king, would you want your daughter to marry Simpleton?
Why or why not?

(Move 3 spaces.)

What colors were the peddler's caps?

(Move 2 spaces.)

If the two weavers had been confronted about not using the thread, what might they have said?

(Move 3 spaces.)

Name the four Bremen Town Musicians.

(Move 1 space.)

How did the Funny Little Woman earn her fortune?

(Move 2 spaces.)

Suppose Desta had not lost his rope? How might the rope have helped him find his missing pet?

(Move 3 spaces.)

Question	Question
Question	Question
Question	Question
Question	Question

94

The soldiers told the villagers that they had entertained the king. Do you think this was true? Why or why not?

(Move 2 spaces.)

What is meant by the phrase "But the world does not stand still" in the story *Such Is the Way of the World?*

(Move 2 spaces.)

Name at least five ingredients that went into the making of the stone soup.

(Move 3 spaces.)

Was Desta a selfish boy? Why or why not?

(Move 1 space.)

Why didn't the Bremen Town Musicians ever get to Bremen?

(Move 3 spaces.)

What do you think caused the dwarf to have such a rude attitude toward Snow White and Rose Red?

(Move 3 spaces.)

What did the rooster's owner want to do with him?

(Move 1 space.)

Was Ming Lo a very smart man? What makes you think this?

(Move 2 spaces.)

Question	Question
Question	Question
Question	Question
Question	Question

96

Why didn't the emperor's subjects tell him that he was parading down the street with no clothes?

(Move 1 space.)

Explain how you might have felt seeing the bear turn into a prince.

(Move 1 space.)

Who finally commented that the king was not wearing any clothes?

(Move 2 spaces.)

Guess why Mrs. Pig thought it time for her sons to leave home.

(Move 2 spaces.)

Where do you think the peddler got his caps?

(Move 1 space.)

Do you think the little pigs had to pay for their building materials?
Why or why not?
If so, how did they pay?

(Move 3 spaces.)

Which pig was the wisest? Why?

(Move 1 space.)

Guess why Ming Lo and his wife chose to build their home at the foot of the mountain. Give reasons.

(Move 1 space.)

Question

Question

Question

Question

Question

Question

Question

Question

Snow White loses her scissors and you must help her find them. Move back one space.

The cap peddler has lost one of his caps. You must help him look for it. Move back two spaces.

Desta's pet monkey does not come home. You stay out all night to help find him. Lose one turn.

Mother pig chases the wolf with her broom. Move ahead one space.

Rose Red combs the bear's coat and he is very grateful. Move ahead two spaces.

The Funny Little Woman escapes by tricking the *oni* into believing she's a witch. Move ahead two spaces.

You convince the emperor that he is not wearing any clothes. Move ahead one space.

The emperor discovers that he has been tricked and wants to catch the weavers. Move back three spaces.

Chance

Chance

Chance

Chance

Chance

Chance

Chance

Chance

100

Simpleton must think of a way to convince the king that he should marry his daughter. Move back two spaces.

The donkey has found another place for the animals to live. Move ahead two spaces.

Ming Lo has fallen off the mountain. Move back three spaces.

The first two pigs have escaped to their brother's house. Move ahead one space.

The soldiers cannot find three smooth stones for their soup. Move back two spaces.

Ming Lo doesn't give good directions for the backwards dance to his wife. Lose one turn.

The Funny Little Woman has lost her magic paddle. You must help her find it. Go back one space.

The Golden Goose loses one of its feathers. Move back two spaces.

Chance

Chance

Chance

Chance

Chance

Chance

Chance

Chance

102

Third Little Pig

Big Bad Wolf

Evil Dwarf

Snow White

Old Donkey

Peddler

BIBLIOGRAPHY

Andersen, Hans Christian. *The Emperor's New Clothes.* New York: Scholastic, Inc., 1977.

Bishop, Gavin. *The Three Little Pigs.* New York: Ashton Scholastic, LTD., 1989.

Brown, Marcia. *Stone Soup.* New York: Charles Scribner's Sons, 1947

Galdone, Paul. *The Three Little Pigs.* New York: The Seabury Press, 1970.

Grimm, the Brothers. *The Bremen Town Musicians.* Illustrated by Paul Galdone. New York: McGraw-Hill Book Company.

_____. *The Bremen Town Musicians.* Illustrated by James Marshall. New York: Dial Books, 1989.

_____. *The Bremen-Town Musicians.* Illustrated by Ilse Plume. New York: Doubleday & Company, Inc., 1980.

_____. *Folk Tales.* "The Golden Goose." Wisconsin: Western Publishing Company, Inc., 1955.

_____. *Folk Tales.* "Snow White and Rose Red." Wisconsin: Western Publishing Company, Inc., 1955.

_____. *Snow White and Rose Red.* Illustrated by Adrienne Adams. New York: Charles Scribner's Sons, 1964.

Elkin, Benjamin. *Such Is the Way of the World.* New York: Parents' Magazine Press, 1968.

Lobel, Arnold. *Ming Lo Moves the Mountain.* New York: William Morrow & Company, 1982.

Mosel, Arlene. *The Funny Little Woman.* New York: Dutton, 1973.

Slobodkina, Esphyr. *Caps for Sale.* New York: Addison-Wesley, 1968.